THE UNIVERSE

ROCKETS AND SATELLITES

ABDO
Publishing Company

Buddy BOOKS
The Universe

A Buddy Book **by Marcia Zappa**

VISIT US AT
www.abdopublishing.com

Published by ABDO Publishing Company, 8000 West 78th Street, Edina, Minnesota 55439.

Printed in the United States of America, North Mankato, Minnesota.
102010
012011

 PRINTED ON RECYCLED PAPER

Coordinating Series Editor: Rochelle Baltzer
Contributing Editors: Megan M. Gunderson, BreAnn Rumsch, Sarah Tieck
Graphic Design: Maria Hosley
Cover Photograph: *NASA*: Sandra Joseph and Rafael Hernandez.
Interior Photographs/Illustrations: *AP Photo*: AP Photo (pp. 13, 15), Florida Today, Rik Jesse (p. 7), NASA (p. 5), NBCU Photo Bank via AP Images (p. 23); *Getty Images*: Kean Collection (p. 25), Robert Clifford Magis/National Geographic (p. 29), Howard Sochurek/Time Life Pictures (p. 27); *iStockphoto*: ©iStockphoto.com/Cmannphoto (p. 9), ©iStockphoto.com/YasmineV (p. 13); *NASA*: European Space Agency (p. 30), Jim Grossman (p. 23), Jim Grossman September 19, 2008 (p. 12), Sandra Joseph and Rafael Hernandez (p. 11), NASA (p. 23), NASA May 19, 2009 (p. 17); *Photo Researchers, Inc.*: Chris Butler (p. 28), Patrick Landman (p. 15), NASA/Science Source (p. 19), Detlev van Ravensway (p. 7); *Shutterstock*: AND Inc. (p. 15), Stephen Coburn (p. 21), Judy Kennamer (p. 9) Pincasso (p. 21).

Library of Congress Cataloging-in-Publication Data

Zappa, Marcia, 1985-
  Rockets and satellites / Marcia Zappa.
    p. cm. -- (The universe)
  ISBN 978-1-61714-691-6
  1. Rocketry--Juvenile literature. 2. Rockets (Aeronautics)--Juvenile literature. 3. Artificial satellites--Juvenile literature. I. Title.
  TL782.5.Z37 2011
  629.4--dc22

                2010032591

Table Of Contents

Rockets and Satellites

People have observed objects in the night sky for thousands of years. At first, they could only study space from the ground.

Over time, people began dreaming of sending spacecraft into space. The invention of rockets and satellites made this dream come true!

Space is the universe outside Earth's atmosphere. It contains galaxies, stars, planets, and other amazing objects.

A Closer Look

One of the hardest parts of **exploring** space is escaping Earth's **gravity**. To do this, a powerful engine called a rocket is used.

Rockets **launch** spacecraft into space. A spacecraft that **orbits** a space object is called a satellite. Thousands of satellites orbit Earth.

The name *rocket* also refers to spacecraft that use rocket engines.

A satellite launched into space by humans is called an artificial satellite (*above*). A natural satellite is a space object, such as a moon, that orbits a planet.

7

Rocket Power

There are many types of rockets. They are used in different ways. Some rockets **launch** weapons during war. Others are used to study Earth's **atmosphere**.

Large, powerful rockets are used to launch spacecraft. These rockets are called launch vehicles. Rockets called boosters connect to spacecraft for extra power.

Very small rockets are used to shoot fireworks into the sky.

9

Blast Off!

Rockets produce energy by burning propellants. Propellants can be liquid or solid. They are made of a **fuel** and a **chemical** that helps the fuel burn.

Launch
Vehicle

Boosters

Most launch vehicles use liquid propellants.
Most boosters use solid propellants.

Rockets blast off from an area called a launchpad.

Many engines need air to burn **fuel**. But, propellants have everything a rocket engine needs to work. This allows rockets to operate in space, where there is almost no air.

Rockets burn propellants very fast. They are more powerful than any other engines their size. So, rockets need a lot of propellants to work for a short time.

Saturn V was a type of rocket used in the 1960s and 1970s. It burned more than 560,000 gallons (2,120,000 L) of propellants in less than three minutes! That amount of fuel would nearly fill an Olympic-sized pool!

Circling Around

Space has many **artificial** satellites. For a satellite to stay in **orbit**, its speed must be just right. If the satellite travels too fast, it will fly off into space. If it moves too slow, **gravity** will cause it to fall from orbit.

A satellite can remain in orbit for many years.

Satellite **orbits** have different shapes. Some are shaped like circles. Others are egg shaped.

Some satellites stay low and close to the space object they circle. Others fly high above it. The higher a satellite is, the longer it takes to orbit the space object.

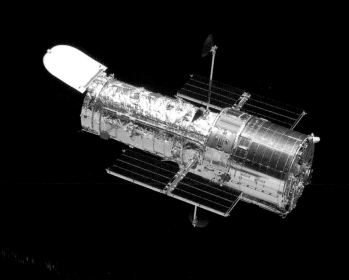

The Hubble Space Telescope is about 350 miles (560 km) above Earth. It takes 97 minutes to orbit Earth one time.

17

Space Probes

Artificial satellites are carried into space by rockets. The two types of artificial satellites are space probes and piloted spacecraft.

Space probes fly without a pilot. Many are sent into **orbit**. These satellites carry cameras and other tools to collect data. They send the data back to Earth.

Space probes have orbited the moon (*below*), the sun, and the planets Venus, Mars, and Jupiter.

Most space probes **orbit** Earth. They do many important jobs. Some observe space. Others observe Earth, its **atmosphere**, and its weather.

Space probes also help send messages around Earth. Many send Internet, radio, television, and telephone messages. Still others help with mapping and directions.

Satellites orbiting Earth send messages to cell phones (*left*) and mapping tools (*below*).

Manned Flights

Piloted spacecraft can also be satellites. Often, they **orbit** a space object while **astronauts** work.

Space capsules, space shuttles, and space stations are three types of piloted spacecraft. In these, astronauts have orbited Earth and the moon.

The first astronauts traveled in space capsules.

Around the 1970s, scientists created the space shuttle. It had wings, so it could land on Earth like an airplane.

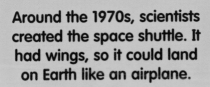

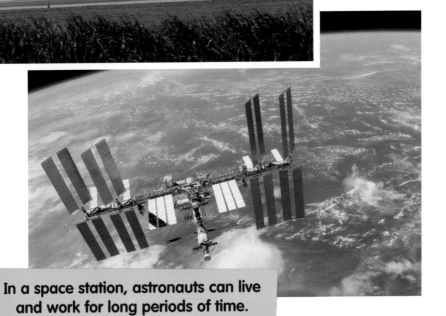

In a space station, astronauts can live and work for long periods of time.

Early Rockets

Rockets have been around for hundreds of years. Many historians believe the Chinese first used rockets during a war in the 1200s.

Over the years, people continued to use rockets for war. After **World War II**, scientists began planning a way to use rockets to **explore** space.

The British used rockets in the War of 1812. The famous line, "and the rockets' red glare," in the U.S. national anthem is based on this.

The Space Age

The first successful space **launch** took place in 1957. The Soviet Union used a rocket to send a satellite to **orbit** Earth.

Then in 1961, a rocket launched a space capsule carrying the first human into space. Soviet **astronaut** Yuri Gagarin orbited Earth one time.

Over the years, many countries sent rockets and satellites into space. Others still hope to do this.

On October 4, 1957, the Soviet Union launched the satellite *Sputnik 1*. It was the first spacecraft to reach space. This was exciting for scientists and people around the world!

Fact Trek

Some rocket engines get as hot as 6000°F (3300°C)!

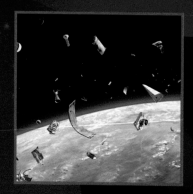

Space contains pieces of used rockets and spacecraft. This is called space junk. When space junk **orbits** a space object, it is considered a satellite.

When a satellite **orbiting** Earth falls, it enters the **atmosphere**. This makes it very hot. Many satellites become so hot they burn up!

A satellite carrying astronauts is built so the inside does not become too hot.

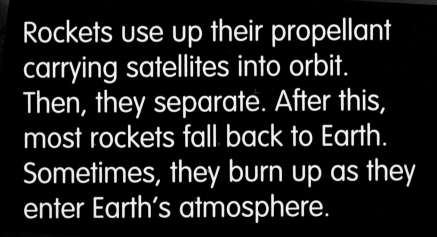

Rockets use up their propellant carrying satellites into orbit. Then, they separate. After this, most rockets fall back to Earth. Sometimes, they burn up as they enter Earth's atmosphere.

Voyage to Tomorrow

Today, scientists are working to make lighter rockets and safer propellants. They also want to create a reusable rocket for **launching** satellites. They hope new rockets and satellites will help them learn even more about space.

There are about 3,000 working satellites orbiting Earth.

Important Words

artificial (ahrt-uh-FIHSH-uhl) made by humans.

astronaut a person who is trained for space travel.

atmosphere (AT-muh-sfihr) the layer of gases that surrounds a space object.

chemical (KEH-mih-kuhl) a substance that can cause reactions and changes.

explore to go into in order to make a discovery or to have an adventure.

fuel (FYOOL) something burned to give heat or power.

gravity a natural force that pulls toward the center of a space object. It also pulls space objects toward each other.

launch to send off with force.

orbit the path of a space object as it moves around another space object. To orbit is to follow this path.

World War II a war fought in Europe, Asia, and Africa from 1939 to 1945.

Web Sites

To learn more about **rockets and satellites** visit ABDO Publishing Company online. Web sites about **rockets and satellites** are featured on our Book Links page. These links are routinely monitored and updated to provide the most current information available.

www.abdopublishing.com

INDEX